# REBEL GiRLS

# EMPOWERiNG THE FUTURE OF STEM

## Changemakers with Disabilities

In partnership with

Rebel Girls, Inc.
421 Elm Ave.
Larkspur, CA 94939
www.rebelgirls.com

Text by Sarah Parvis
Cover illustrations (left to right, top to bottom): Jo Dertili, Lively Scout, Elizabeth Montero Santa, Lucy Rogers, Rubii Red
Cover design by Georgia Rucker
Special thanks to the Rebel Girls team: Amy Pfister, Anjelika Temple, Annie Liu, Denise Gomez-Rivera, Emma May-Bradley, Haley Dapkus, Inky Son, Isadora Manzaro, Jes Wolfe, Michon Vanderpoel, Natalie Hara, Rachel Toby

10 9 8 7 6 5 4 3 2 1

ISBN: 979-8-88964-167-4

# CONTENTS



## BONUS! AUDiO STORY!

Scan the code, and you'll be whisked away on an audio adventure, where you will hear a longer story about Wanda Diaz-Merced (page 30). Enjoy!

**The Royal Australian Chemical Institute (RACI)** is proud to present this book in partnership with Rebel Girls. Together, we have sought to create a resource that not only inspires but also reflects the diverse realities of children who may be considering a future in STEM. Too often, young people with disabilities lack access to visible role models who share their experiences. This book helps address that gap by sharing the stories of remarkable women whose achievements demonstrate that a career in STEM is not only possible, but within reach.

I'm proud that we've taken this step towards greater equity, diversity, and inclusion in STEM.

RACI recognises that many challenges still prevent children with disabilities from fully accessing opportunities in STEM. These challenges may be physical, educational, or cultural, but their impact is clear – they limit participation, representation, and visibility. We believe that equity, diversity, and inclusion are not just values to aspire to, but essential elements for innovation and progress.

Supporting children with disabilities to see themselves in STEM is not simply a matter of fairness, it is a matter of unlocking the creativity, resilience, and potential they already possess.

This book is a celebration of brilliant women with disabilities who are making important contributions to STEM and society. Their stories stand as powerful examples for the next generation, and we thank them for generously sharing their journeys and lived experiences.

The Royal Australian Chemical Institute remains committed to championing diversity and inclusion across the STEM landscape. I see this book as one step in a broader journey – towards a future where every child can imagine themselves as part of the STEM community.

**Shenal Basnayake**
CEO, Royal Australian Chemical Institute

# • INTRODUCTiON •

**Every young person** deserves to see a representation of themselves in the pages of a book. When girls – and especially girls with disabilities – see role models who look like them, live like them, and dream like them, they may begin to understand that their own future is limitless.

This collaboration between the Royal Australian Chemical Institute (RACI) and Rebel Girls is more than a collection of stories. It is a celebration of brilliant women in science, technology, engineering, and mathematics who are reshaping our world, and a reminder that diversity is not just important – it is vital. It is the catalyst for innovation and progress. The women in this book represent courage, curiosity, and resilience. They prove that talent knows no boundaries, and that the strength of STEM lies in the richness of perspectives it embraces.

For too long, systemic barriers have told some children that STEM isn't for them. This book seeks to change that narrative. By sharing stories of women with disabilities who have pursued their passions and thrived, we hope to show young readers that STEM belongs to everyone – and so do its opportunities.

At the RACI, we are passionate about opening doors for young people to see themselves in chemistry. Chemistry is the science of transformation – of elements combining in new ways to create something greater – and we believe the same is true when diverse voices and perspectives come together. Through this initiative, we want to show that there is no single path to success in STEM. In these pages, you will read about how Susanna Cramb is using statistics to improve people's health, how Alise Fox is using maths to support sustainable fishing, and how Katrina Wruck is using chemistry to protect the environment.

Whether you envision yourself in the classroom like Natasha Ward, in the lab like Jiao Jiao Li, or out in the community like Verity Normington, know that there are countless options open to you.

To every girl reading this: your ideas matter, your voice matters, and your future in STEM is yours to claim. May these stories inspire you to be bold, ask questions, and believe that you belong in any space you choose to enter.

**Amanda Ellis**

President, Royal Australian Chemical Institute

# • ALiSE FOX •

## FiSHERiES SCiENTiST AND SCiENCE COMMUNiCATOR

**S**itting in her maths classroom one day, Alise felt a fluttery feeling in her stomach. Her teacher was talking about equations and how the relationships between numbers could explain almost anything. Suddenly they'd moved from addition and multiplication to unlocking the secrets of the universe. And that fluttery feeling? That was excitement.

Alise always loved nature. Together with her mum, she'd scamper around the beach or the rainforest, inspecting shells and marvelling at all the funky fungi they could find. Nature is enormous. And yet, she realised, she could zoom in and see networks of relationships. Zooming in further, she could see the chemical reactions that make up biological occurrences . . . which follow the laws of physics . . . which can be explained using logic and numbers. There was that fluttery feeling again!

*How could she turn her interests into a career?* she wondered. The only person she knew who made a career out of maths was her teacher. So she became a maths teacher! But it wasn't the job for her. Back to uni she went. She explored lots of exciting topics, and eventually, she found a job that combines her love of maths and nature. As a fisheries scientist, she uses maths to figure out how many fish are in the ocean, which helps others write laws aimed at keeping the ocean healthy.

Sometimes at school or work, Alise would feel sad or frustrated when she compared herself to her friends or colleagues. At 32 years old, she found out that she is neurodivergent. Her autism and ADHD are part of what makes her unique. "I have a different kind of brain!" she says.

She's found tactics to help her stay focused, such as taking breaks, swapping paper books for audiobooks, and keeping fidget toys on her desk. Alise's advice to everyone, especially neurodivergent folks, is: "Learn about yourself, trust that the way you think is perfectly valid, and give yourself whatever tools you need."

BORN 1992

AUSTRALiA

"EXPECT TWISTS AND TURNS
BECAUSE STEM IS HUGE AND IT'S
EVOLVING. THE JOB YOU END UP IN
MIGHT NOT EVEN EXIST YET."
—ALISE FOX

ILLUSTRATION BY
SAMI BAYLY

# CATHY FOLEY

PHYSICIST AND SCIENCE ADVOCATE

One day, Cathy turned on her family's black-and-white TV. The hosts of *Summer School of Science* were busy doing experiments. Magnets? Sound waves? Electricity? It was like watching magic in action!

Cathy loved puzzles. The idea that invisible forces could shape the world thrilled her! She enjoyed exploring the mysteries of nature. But then a teacher said something that Cathy would never forget. She said that Cathy wasn't smart enough to be a scientist. It felt like she'd been punched in the gut.

She stopped and thought about those horrible, hurtful words. Cathy is dyslexic. It was true that she read a little more slowly than some of her classmates. Sometimes she swapped letters around when she was writing her school assignments. Her brain worked differently from a lot of other kids'. Her dyslexia was part of what made her quick, clever mind special and what fuelled her sense of wonder.

So she made an important decision: She would not let this ignorant woman's words hold her back. She would push harder, learn more, and pursue her interests. With hard work and the help of some awesome mentors, she found strategies for learning and communicating that worked for her.

At Macquarie University, Cathy earned her PhD in physics and became a researcher. On one exciting project, she helped discover how to use superconducting technology to locate mineral deposits deep underground. On another, she used physics to make advances in medical imaging.

In 2021, she became Australia's chief scientist. She advised the government on science and technology, and helped to weave scientific innovation into the list of the nation's priorities. "It was an extraordinary privilege," she said, "to amplify the voices of researchers and show young people what's possible in science."

BORN 1957
AUSTRALIA

"THERE WERE MANY TIMES WHEN I WAS
UNDERESTIMATED OR EXCLUDED. IT GAVE ME
A DETERMINATION TO CHANGE THE SYSTEM,
SO THE NEXT GENERATION OF WOMEN –
AND ESPECIALLY GIRLS WHO FEEL LIKE
OUTSIDERS – WILL HAVE A CLEARER PATH."
–CATHY FOLEY
ILLUSTRATION BY
VERONICA GUARINO

PALAEONTOLOGiST

"Fifty million years ago, whales and dolphins lived on land," a voice explained. "Over time, their limbs shrank, and their tails grew wider and more powerful . . ."  At nine years old, Eleanor stared at the screen. Her eyes were wide, and her brain was buzzing as the narrator described how whales and dolphins left land behind to live in the sea.

This video introduced Eleanor to palaeontology, the study of fossilised animals and plants. It also changed her life.

Eleanor was born with a rare condition called spinal muscular atrophy. It causes extreme muscle weakness and difficulty breathing. Using technology such as a power wheelchair and speech-to-text software, she has studied marine biology and become a journalist. Now, she's getting her master's degree in palaeontology. She's using her sharp mind and keen powers of observation to explore what plant and animal fossils can tell us about life in the past.

Uncovering ancient fossils often takes place in remote places with rugged terrain. It is not a wheelchair-friendly activity! With help from some dedicated family and friends, Eleanor went on a dig in 2016. On her first day, she found a perfectly preserved seashell that had turned into black opal over 110 million years. "It was such an amazing rush," she said, "when I saw it gleaming in a pile of rubble resting on my wheelchair tray."

Going on the dig was exciting. But Eleanor can do her research from home. She analyses super-high-resolution scans of ancient specimens on her computer. In this way, she identifies new species and helps build clearer pictures of what life was like millions of years ago.

Just as whales and dolphins underwent a major transformation so long ago, science and technology are always evolving. As Eleanor pursues her dream career, she will be right there, using exciting new tools to contribute to science.

BORN 1993

AUSTRALiA

"WOMEN CAN DO ANYTHING THEY WANT, AND SO CAN PEOPLE WITH DISABILITIES. THE MORE OF US WHO ARE CHANGING THE WORLD, THE BETTER THE FUTURE WILL BE."
—ELEANOR BEIDATSCH
ILLUSTRATION BY JOANNE DERTILI

# • FARiDA BEDWEi •

SOFTWARE ENGiNEER

Farida was a clever, curious child. She invented scenarios for her Barbies, raced remote-controlled cars, and never left the house without a book.

Farida was born in Nigeria. Her family moved around a bit before settling in Ghana when she was nine. When her mum tried to register Farida for school though, she hit a wall. Farida has cerebral palsy, a condition that affects balance and body movement, and none of the schools in the area would admit her.

After a few years of home-schooling, they tried again. Her junior high was not accessible, but her friends helped her walk from the car to her classroom. Senior high was much less accessible. So Farida forged a different path. She enrolled in a computer course at a nearby technology centre. She was the youngest student there, but she was determined to earn the highest scores.

With an IT diploma in hand, she went to a local software company. "I don't have any experience," she said, "but if you give me a chance, I promise you'll never regret it." While working part-time, she earned a second diploma. Then she completed her computer science degree at a university in the UK.

Later, she cofounded a company and developed a cloud software platform that helped finance companies provide micro loans. At Microsoft, she worked on a metaverse project, helping to build features, such as the ability to teleport and appear in a room full of avatars. Now she uses her top-notch computer skills to help young people – especially young women – thrive in a rapidly changing digital world.

Farida has also created a comic starring Karmzah, a superheroine with cerebral palsy who gets her powers from her crutches. She wants all children with disabilities, especially those who use assistive devices, to feel powerful and be proud of their accomplishments.

BORN 1979

NiGERiA AND GHANA

ILLUSTRATION BY
ELIZABETH MONTERO SANTA
"WITH THE RISE AND FAST
EVOLUTION OF AI, THE
POSSIBILITIES ARE ENDLESS,
AND I'D LOVE TO EXPLORE
HOW IT IS BEING USED TO
FACILITATE INCLUSIVE
LEARNING FOR CHILDREN
WITH DISABILITIES."
—FARIDA BEDWEI

# • JiAO JiAO Li •

## BiOMEDiCAL ENGiNEER

Jiao Jiao didn't really know what engineering was when she entered university. But she quickly knew she'd made the right choice. She absolutely loved uncovering the secrets of how things work!

Once, during her second year at university, she found out that her family planned to put up a satellite dish. Immediately, she drew up a diagram and began to calculate the forces that would act on the dish. She wanted to make sure the dish would be safe in any kind of weather – even gale-force winds. Her engineering training was already paying off!

Jiao Jiao graduated with degrees in biomedical engineering and medical science. Soon, she was focusing on regenerative medicine. She combines cutting-edge nanotechnology with cell biology, materials science, computer science, and medicine to create options for treating disease. She and her colleagues are growing new organs and body parts to replace damaged ones.

As they age, many people develop bone and joint diseases. It makes it hard for them to get around, and it can be very painful. Seeing members of her own family grapple with these conditions has inspired Jiao Jiao to do everything she can to help people age better, so they can live their lives to the fullest.

Jiao Jiao knows about living with pain. She suffers from a medical condition called endometriosis. She often adjusts her lifestyle and work arrangements to manage her symptoms. She wishes more people understood that many disabilities are invisible, and that there are some simple things we can do to make life and work more comfortable for a lot of people.

Looking ahead, Jiao Jiao is full of hope. She says, "We are at the brink of building whole organs, robotic devices to replace body parts, and cures for previously intractable diseases." The future is bright!

BORN 1987

CHiNA AND AUSTRALiA

"IF THERE ARE NOT A LOT OF PEOPLE WHO LOOK LIKE YOU IN THE FIELD YOU WANT TO GET INTO, BE BOLD AND BE THAT PERSON YOU WANT TO BECOME."
—JIAO JIAO LI
ILLUSTRATION BY
LILY NIE

## INDUSTRiAL CHEMiST

Once upon a time, a girl named Katrina curled up on the sofa to watch a movie. In it, Nicolas Cage played a biochemist who works for the FBI and saves the world from a chemical attack. "How cool is that?!" she thought, "To save the world using science!" She worked hard and found her own way to make her mark. Today, she uses chemistry to protect the environment. "I still get to help save the planet," she says, "just with fewer explosions."

When she first started studying science, she had to commute four hours a day to the university. It was exhausting! So after a few months, she moved to Brisbane, where she lived in a share house and continued her studies. It was *a lot* of work, and it was tough to find the money to live on her own. But she followed her curiosity and earned her PhD in sustainable process engineering.

Later, Katrina was researching the rocks that are left over from mining. "Instead of treating them as waste," she wondered, "what if I could turn them into something useful?" She jumped into action and developed a process to transform these rocks into the main ingredient in laundry detergent.

Her product does more than keep clothing clean. It improves people's health. Rheumatic heart disease is caused by bacteria, and people who don't have access to laundry facilities and detergent have higher rates of it. In Australia, the disease disproportionately affects Indigenous communities. She realised she was onto something big!

Katrina is a proud Panaylayg woman (Zenadth Kes). She is also neurodivergent. Over the years, some close-minded people have underestimated her or even discriminated against her. Instead of believing those voices, she says, "I let them fuel my fire, and I am determined to prove them wrong." She's excited to continue battling forever chemicals and inspiring the next generation of STEM leaders.

BORN 1994

**AUSTRALiA**

"IF EVERYTHING WENT PERFECTLY THE FIRST TIME, THERE'D BE NOTHING TO LEARN. MISTAKES AREN'T SETBACKS — THEY'RE STEPPING STONES TO SOMETHING EXTRAORDINARY."
—KATRINA WRUCK
ILLUSTRATION BY RUBII RED

# KiOWA SCOTT-HURLEY

## AI AND CYBERSECURiTY SPECiALiST

**L**ate at night, young Kiowa was usually busy, fighting fictional battles in magical universes or brushing up on cat breeds with her handy encyclopedias. Whether she was devouring books, making art, or writing stories, she was always exercising her creativity.

Growing up in Gunai Kurnai Country, there wasn't a lot of money to go around. Kiowa and her best friend came up with their own clever ways to patch the holes in their shoes and entertain themselves with what they had on hand.

It was rare for kids from her area to go to uni, but she did. And she began to study maths and philosophy. Kiowa had always been bright and open-minded, but along the way, she realised that she'd made some assumptions about scientists that weren't always true. *People who worked in STEM,* she thought, *wore white coats and spent their days quietly toiling in a lab. Right?*

Today, Kiowa provides guidance to scientists and everyday people about how to avoid risks and use AI smartly. She also manages a team of engineers who use her findings to build new AI tools. She spends her days at a computer, she still gets to use her art skills, and she is constantly collaborating with others. And there are no lab coats to be found in her wardrobe!

Computers are amazing tools, but people are invaluable. They provide different perspectives that help hone ideas and push them forwards. Kiowa brings her perspectives to everything she does. She's a Dja Dja Wurrung woman, and she has a chronic illness. Her experiences help her notice things that other people don't.

"Instead of assuming things are already awesome," she says, "I'm always wondering how things could be better – and that's a real skill to have in STEM!"

BORN 1998

AUSTRALiA

"I ALWAYS TRY TO REMEMBER HOW MY UNIQUE PERSPECTIVE MAKES ME A BETTER SCIENTIST, INSTEAD OF FOCUSING ON HOW IT RESTRICTS ME."
—KIOWA SCOTT-HURLEY
ILLUSTRATION BY SAMANTHA CAMPBELL

# MADDY LAHM

## MARINE CHEMIST

**O**nce upon a time, there was a high school student named Maddy who failed an open-book test in chemistry and grew up to be . . . a marine chemist!

When Maddy and her brother were little, they'd romp around the wetlands near their home, helping turtles cross the road and searching storm drains for frog eggs. Later, she'd relax on the beach, or kayak with her family.

She always felt at home by the water, so it was no surprise that she grew up to work on a science vessel at sea. What was a surprise – at least to her high school chem teacher – is that she majored in chemistry at university! It's true that she originally struggled with the subject, but Maddy had a professor at uni who made her look at chemistry in a whole new way.

Maddy was also interested in genetics and medicine. Because of a rare genetic mutation, she and her brother were born deaf. As a baby, she received a cochlear implant, a medical device that connects an external hearing aid to her auditory nerve and allows her to hear. Learning about genetics and the human body helped Maddy learn more about herself. "I thought of myself as a cool science experiment," she said.

Today, Maddy spends about three months a year at sea, living and working aboard a research ship. Her team collects samples of seawater from depths of 6,000 metres, and collaborates with other scientists to monitor change in the oceans and reveal information about aquatic life. She has also helped to design and build Hydrobox, the world's first portable hydrochemistry laboratory.

As a seagoing scientist, Maddy is constantly learning. She's having an exciting, fulfilling career, and she's opening more doors for women and people with disabilities who are under-represented in her field. Hopefully not for long!

BORN 1997

UNiTED STATES

"I LOVE BEING ABLE TO CONTRIBUTE TO AN ONGOING EFFORT TO REDEFINE WHAT EXCELLENCE IN SCIENCE LOOKS LIKE."
—MADDY LAHM
MADDY
ILLUSTRATION BY LUCY ROGERS

# NATASHA WARD

## TEACHER

**B**y the time Natasha's youngest brother was five years old, he was singing the periodic table song with confidence. That's because Natasha taught it to him. In biology class, she noticed the girls sitting behind her were struggling. So she jumped in to help. Photosynthesis, animal habitats, genetics – she loved it all and wanted her classmates to understand it like she did. Natasha followed her love of science and her love of teaching to become . . . a science teacher!

In one position, she worked on a project to weave First Nations science into the primary school curriculum. In one lesson, she and her students looked at the four western seasons and the seven seasons of the Wurundjeri Woi Wurrung peoples. These traditional seasons don't follow calendar dates. Instead, they correspond to changes in the environment.

Later, she led school excursions for students across Victoria. She got to introduce students to snakes, turtles, stick insects, lizards, sugar gliders, and even potoroos! It was a joy to show students that the animals – even the lizards! – had their own distinct personalities. Natasha was in her element as she taught about everything from ancient megafauna to analysing DNA during crime scene investigations.

Today, she is an academic coordinator for the Young Indigenous Women's STEM Academy. A proud Indigenous woman herself, she supports girls in high school and helps them find STEM opportunities that match their interests.

Empowering Indigenous girls is important to Natasha, and so is looking out for young people who may be struggling with health issues. She has ADHD and chronic health conditions. She know what it feels like when pain makes it hard to get out of bed. So she supports others, with patience and understanding, and helps them build the confidence they need to thrive in school and beyond.

ILLUSTRATiON BY
RUBii RED
"OUR ANCESTORS HAVE DONE STEM FOR
THOUSANDS OF YEARS, AND THERE ARE
INDiGENOUS PEOPLE MAKiNG A PATH
FOR YOU TO DO iT TOO. GO AND SHOW
THE WORLD HOW DEADLY YOU ARE!"
—NATASHA WARD

# SUSANNA CRAMB



Sustainability was the name of the game for Susanna's family. Growing up, they planted crops and raised animals, so they'd always have fresh milk and eggs. And young Susanna spent plenty of time outdoors, caring for chickens and ducks and helping the littlest ducklings catch up. She pored over science magazines and did experiments in the living room. Young Susanna put caterpillars in shoeboxes – with the right kinds of leaves and plenty of air holes, of course! She'd watch as the caterpillars formed chrysalises and eventually emerged as butterflies. Then, she'd carefully release them back into nature.

When it came to career options, veterinarian was definitely on Susanna's list. But she wanted to help people too. So she studied medical science and then got a master's degree in public health and tropical medicine. That degree introduced her to two fields that would become the cornerstones of her career: epidemiology and biostatistics! Epidemiologists study the causes and patterns of disease. And biostatisticians use data to analyse things, such as health trends and whether medicines are working. A wheelchair user herself, she found a way to use her maths skills to help other people with health conditions.

Susanna's current projects are aimed at improving diabetes and cancer outcomes across Australia, heart health among Aboriginal and Torres Strait Islander peoples, access to healthy food, and outcomes for emergency medical treatment. The variety of projects is super exciting. So is the thrill of discovery! While analysing data, there are moments when she has knowledge that no one else has. Then she creates visuals with that data, writes reports, mentors students, speaks at conferences, and shares what she learns so people can use the data to make the world a better, healthier place.

She says: "When people come together with purpose and combine their expertise, amazing things happen!"

BORN 1980

AUSTRALIA

"DEVELOP YOUR COMMUNICATION SKILLS, CURIOSITY, AND CREATIVITY — THESE ATTRIBUTES ARE SO IMPORTANT IN STEM!"
—SUSANNA CRAMB
ILLUSTRATION BY ELIZABETH MONTERO SANTA

# • VERiTY NORMiNGTON •



"**I**n central Australia, surrounded by tens of kilometres of flat, dusty plains with clusters of mulga trees, there is a jagged range of red and purple rocks," says Verity. She's telling the story of diamictite. This fascinating rock was formed from all sorts of rocks and minerals that were crushed and buried by glaciers then pushed back to the surface of the Earth after many hundreds of millions of years. And many years after that, Verity discovered her love for geology and storytelling.

Verity didn't think much of it when she picked the geology class. She'd been ill and missed a lot of school. After failing year 12 and taking some time off to get well, she enrolled in an adult education college. Maths and science had always been interesting to her, so she thought she'd give geology a try. Within three weeks, she was obsessed. She'd found her path, and it was paved with rocks!

She got her PhD and spent seven years mapping the Amadeus Basin. She roamed the desert, describing the rocks she found, creating maps of the area, and unravelling the history and mysteries of the landscape.

Over time, she realised how much she loved advocating for science – taking difficult scientific concepts and explaining them in ways that everyone can understand. She also found a passion for speaking up for minority groups, like those with chronic illnesses.

When Verity was 18, she finally got a diagnosis for what had been making her ill for years. It was Crohn's disease, which causes inflammation in the digestive tract. Throughout her life, she's had to take months off school or work to heal or recover from surgeries. And while that has been difficult, she also sees what her illness has taught her. "It's made me a better leader," she says. It's increased her empathy for others and taught her to be prepared. "It has taught me to be flexible and go with the flow," says Verity. "It has shown me how strong I truly am."

"GEOSCiENCE iS FULL OF AHA MOMENTS – iT'S WHY I DO iT! I AM CONSTANTLY LEARNiNG. WHEN YOU FiNALLY FiGURE OUT HOW A ROCK OR LANDFORM FiTS iNTO THE GREATER PiCTURE, iT'S ALWAYS A GREAT FEELING."
—VERiTY NORMiNGTON
ILLUSTRATiON BY VERONiCA GUARiNO

# WANDA DiAZ-MERCED



**E**ven though she didn't have a lot of books at home, Wanda loved to read. Once, she found an enormous atlas – and it set her imagination on fire! Because of a developmental disability, her sister stayed mostly in her room. Wanda would climb into bed next to her, and the pair would read sections of the book aloud to one another, painting mental pictures of countless fascinating places far away. Sometimes, Wanda would hold onto imaginary controls and pretend to fly a spacecraft in a whole new galaxy.

When she was teenager, Wanda began to lose her sight. It was frustrating and scary, and it made going to school much more difficult. She was studying for her physics degree when she became completely blind. What should she do? Should she quit? Should she push on? Wanda refused to give up on her studies.

While she was at uni, a friend pulled her aside and introduced her to something incredible: live radio transmissions from space.

"What a horrible noise!" she thought. "What is it?" she asked.

"It is the sound of a solar burst," he responded.

All of a sudden, that awful noise turned into something beautiful – the sound of possibility!

It took her six years, but she got her degree. Then she applied for an internship at NASA. Soon she began using sonification. This is a process that converts data into sound waves instead of visual displays. Wanda helped develop existing software so it would interpret data better than before – and make astronomy accessible to scientists who'd been left out in the past. Eventually, she proved that audible data increases astronomers' ability to detect black holes.

Wanda is dedicated to improving the ways people analyse astronomical data, and she's passionate about inviting more people into STEM.

She reminds us all: "Science is for everyone."

PUERTO RiCO

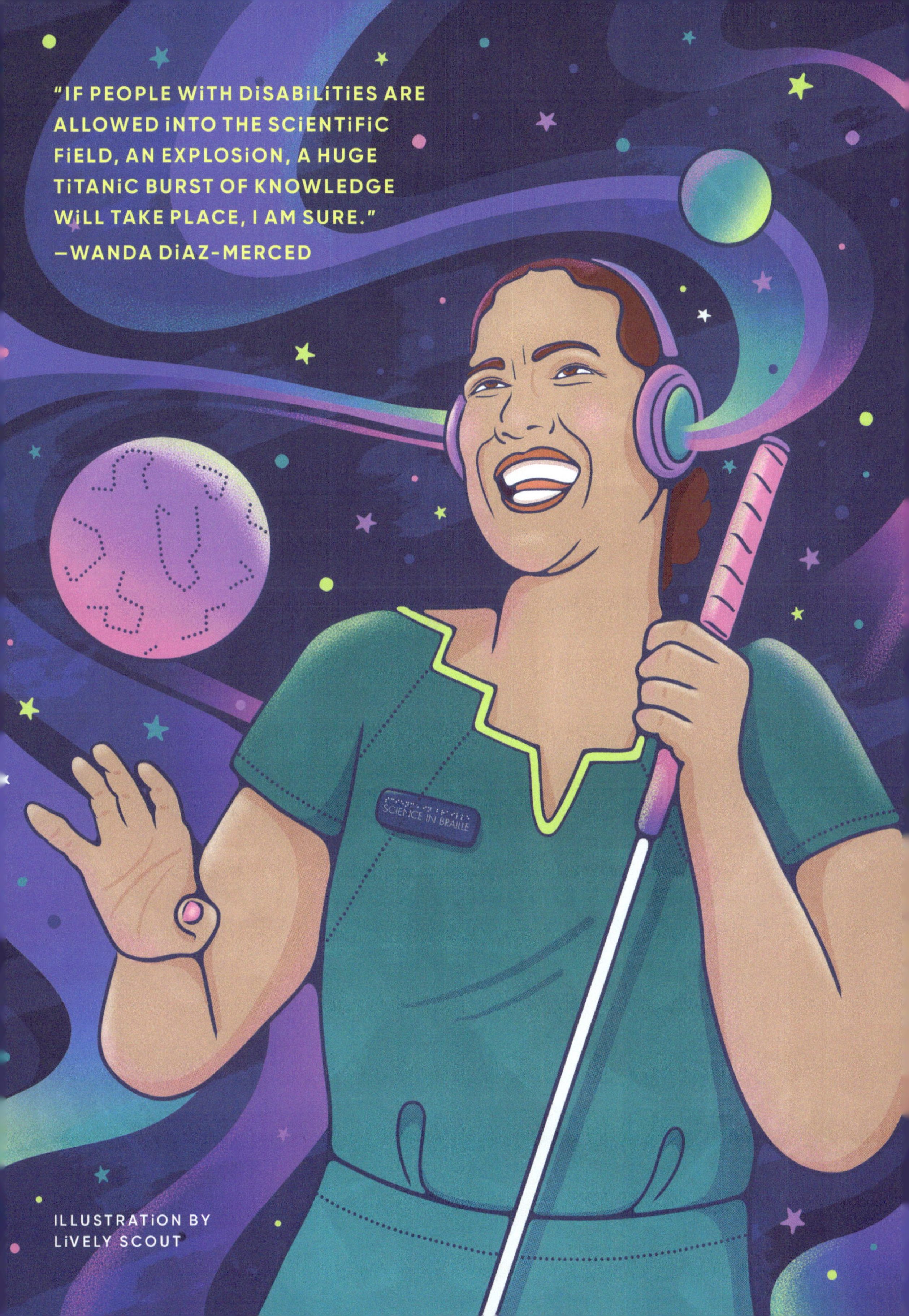

"IF PEOPLE WiTH DiSABiLiTiES ARE ALLOWED iNTO THE SCiENTiFiC FiELD, AN EXPLOSiON, A HUGE TiTANiC BURST OF KNOWLEDGE WiLL TAKE PLACE, I AM SURE."
—WANDA DiAZ-MERCED
SCIENCE IN BRAILLE
ILLUSTRATION BY LiVELY SCOUT

# IN THEiR OWN WORDS

## WHAT ADViCE DO YOU HAVE FOR YOUNG NEURODiVERGENT PEOPLE?

"Spend some time looking inside your own brain and think about what works for you. No two brains are the same, especially for neurodivergent folk. Learn about yourself and trust that the way you think is perfectly valid, and give yourself whatever tools you need. Also, choosing one particular pathway as a career doesn't mean you can't make time for other interests and hobbies as they arise."

—ALiSE FOX

"Find what works for you. The way you do something may not be the same as your friends, but you are working to your strengths, just like they are working to theirs. You can do whatever you set your mind to, in your own beautiful way."

—NATASHA WARD

"Your disability does not define your limits. It may make the path different, but it can also make you stronger and more innovative."

—CATHY FOLEY

"Look for the alternate paths. Your disability or illness doesn't have to define who you are and what your future looks like. If people say you can't do something in the traditional way, find the non-traditional way to do it."

**—VERiTY NORMiNGTON**

"Don't be afraid to talk about it – it's hard, but together we can make a difference and make it easier for others like us."

**—JiAO JiAO Li**

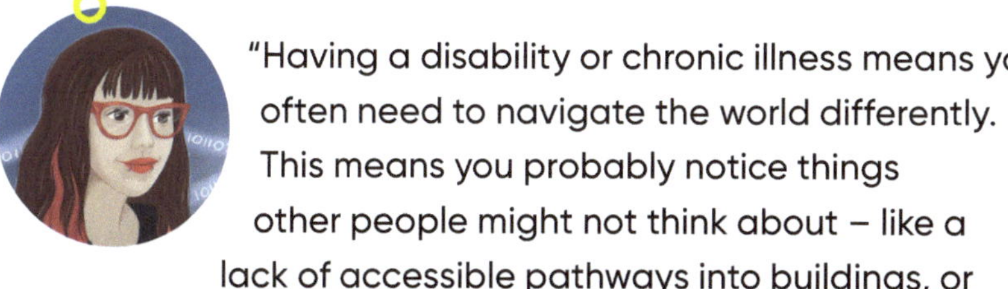

# WHAT ADViCE DO YOU HAVE FOR YOUNG PEOPLE WITH DiSABiLiTiES?

"Having a disability or chronic illness means you often need to navigate the world differently. This means you probably notice things other people might not think about – like a lack of accessible pathways into buildings, or kitchen utensils that are difficult to use with mobility issues. While it can be tiring always noticing how the world hasn't accounted for you, it teaches you how to be creative when overcoming these challenges, and teaches you to look for opportunities for the world to be different. That's where innovation and improvement happens."

**—KiOWA SCOTT-HURLEY**

"You can dream big – your voice matters!"

**—SUSANNA CRAMB**

"We are actually just like everybody else, we just have body or brain part(s) that don't function as that of the majority."

**—FARiDA BEDWEi**

"I wish more people understood that disabilities can be invisible, and that any chronic condition (both physical and mental) that prevents someone from living a normal life or achieving their 100 per cent can be a disability."

**—JiAO JiAO Li**

## WHAT DO YOU WiSH PEOPLE UNDERSTOOD ABOUT NEURODiVERSE PEOPLE OR PEOPLE WiTH DiSABiLiTiES OR CHRONiC iLLNESSES?

"Not all disabilities and illnesses are static or visible. I have a chronic illness which means sometimes I need to use a walking stick to help with my balance and fatigue, but other times I can walk around without it. A lot of people assume that I'm 'all better' if they see me without it, when I have a permanent illness that has different support needs depending on how unwell I am and what activities I am doing. I also think it's important to ask people what they need instead of assuming for them. My walking stick is a mobility aid which enables me to keep doing activities that might be too difficult without it. It's best to not assume how my illness restricts my activities, and to politely ask instead."

**—KiOWA SCOTT-HURLEY**

"That difference is not a deficit. Neurodiverse people often bring unique strengths, perspectives, and creativity. Given the right support, they can thrive."

**—CATHY FOLEY**

"We are humans, just like everyone else! We don't need to be idolised nor victimised."

**—SUSANNA CRAMB**

"We are just as clever, motivated, and capable of doing a job or studying as anyone else. You shouldn't see people with disabilities as weak or unhappy because we look different to you. People with disabilities can do anything we want to do, we just need understanding and support when a task is more difficult for us than it is for other people. We can still be the best person for the job."

**—ELEANOR BEiDATSCH**

"ADHD isn't always boys running around the classroom unable to sit still. The girl who chats a lot in class and gets distracted easily can be struggling just as much. But we can do whatever we put our minds to. Our brains mean we can see things in new ways and can be incredibly creative because of how quickly we can think. Learning to work with my ADHD rather than masking it has allowed me to thrive – my ADHD is my superpower."

**—NATASHA WARD**

"My inclusion increases teamwork. During a job interview, I once explained that the extra effort it takes to include me as a deaf employee also helps ensure that everyone understands their tasks/roles and the directions in preparation for jobs. If we are to begin addressing barriers to accessibility and inclusion within marine sciences, we should recognise that these efforts help the abled as well — hand signals on boats can be a useful resource when even those with good hearing can't hear over wind or machinery. Efforts intended for inclusivity can become more intentional efforts towards maximum safety."

**—MADDY LAHM**

"We are not lazy, naughty, rude, or incapable of doing things. We just have a different type of brain that is not necessarily accounted for in the world that's been built around us. The more we normalise the ways that we are different, the more room there will be in society for all types of brains."

**—ALiSE FOX**

"STEM careers are awesome – you will be fascinated in unimaginable ways about what is possible and what you can do to help the world become a better place."

**—JiAO JiAO Li**

"Get out there and do it! The world needs your experiences and ideas to solve the big challenges of today and the future. Once you start telling people what it is you are passionate about, you will find the people that are your cheerleaders and the people that are interested in the same things as you. Hold onto those people, and ignore the nay-sayers."

**—VERiTY NORMiNGTON**

## WHAT ADViCE DO YOU HAVE FOR YOUNG WOMEN TODAY WHO ARE iNTERESTED iN STEM?

"If you feel like you want to know how the world works, how life evolved, why there are so many planets in the sky, or how climate change will affect your future, then no barrier or prejudice should hold you back. You might have to overcome more difficulties than other people in the same career as you, but remember that those barriers are the fault of the people that put them up, not you."

**—ELEANOR BEiDATSCH**

"You don't need to know your whole journey, or where you're going to end up, before you get started. Be curious, and learn about the things that excite you. If you're passionate about something, you can find a way to harness it to save the world."

**—ALiSE FOX**

"Never give up. Seek out good mentors and treasure mentor-disciple relations."
**—WANDA DiAZ-MERCED**

"Look beyond coding. There are other options in technology to explore – like product development, cybersecurity, intellectual property, and computing law. And there's a lot that can be done with agentic AI as well."
**—FARiDA BEDWEi**

"Believe in yourself, even if others doubt you. Find mentors and allies, and don't be afraid to follow your curiosity. The world needs your ideas."
**—CATHY FOLEY**

"Do it! The world is fascinating, and you should follow what interests you. If anyone tells you that you can't or that a topic is for boys, do it anyway. Your curiosity is a strength, and STEM needs more women to give new ideas and perspectives!"
**—NATASHA WARD**

Founded in 1917, the Royal Australian Chemical Institute (RACI) pairs a rich legacy of scientific excellence with a commitment to advancing the chemical sciences for the betterment of Australia and beyond. Our institute is a vibrant community of passionate individuals from education, academia, industry, and government, united by a common purpose: to foster the understanding and application of chemistry for the benefit of society. At the heart of what we do is the pursuit of knowledge, innovation, and collaboration. Please join us on this journey, where knowledge meets innovation, and together, we can shape the future of chemistry. **raci.org.au**

## · ACKNOWLEDGMENTS ·

**THiS BOOK** has been the result of a collective effort. It could not have been made possible without the efforts of the following individuals and organizations.

### RACI

**HANNAH MCCARTHY** – Project Manager (RACI Education, Careers & Outreach Coordinator)

**MARGARET HARTLEY FTSE, FRACI CCHEM, MAICD** – Project Sponsorship Team (Co-Chair RACI Inclusion & Diversity Committee (Jan 2023 – June 2025)

## PRiNCiPAL GOVERNMENT PARTNER

**Australian Government**

**Department of Industry, Science and Resources**

*The views expressed herein are not necessarily the views of the Commonwealth of Australia, and the Commonwealth of Australia does not accept responsibility for any information or advice contained herein.*

## PRiNCiPAL HiGHER EDUCATiON PARTNER

## PARTNERS

### THE UNIVERSITY OF MELBOURNE:

With thanks to the Faculty of Engineering and Information Technology and the School of Chemical and Biomedical Engineering for their support.

### THE UNIVERSITY OF NEW SOUTH WALES:

With thanks to the Divisions of Research & Societal Impact Equity and Engagement and the Pro Vice Chancellor Societal Transformation and Equity for their support.

### DEAKIN UNIVERSITY:

With thanks to the Faculty of Science, Engineering and Built Environment for their support.

This work is supported financially through the Royal Society of Chemistry Inclusion and Diversity Fund. The views expressed herein do not necessarily reflect those of the RSC.

# • ABOUT THE AUTHOR •

**SARAH PARVIS** is a US-based author and editor dedicated to amplifying stories of women and girls doing awesome things in the world. Nothing makes her happier than learning a new fact about an animal behavior, a piece of art, or a quirk of science. She started telling stories at a young age and doesn't plan to stop anytime soon. Sarah has written about haunted houses, nature, women's football, entrepreneurship, girl power, and more – and she can't wait to see what's next!

# • ILLUSTRATiON CREDiTS •

**ELiZABETH MONTERO SANTA, DOMiNiCAN REPUBLiC, 15, 26** Elizabeth is an illustrator from the Dominican Republic who seeks to give more visibility to Black women, women of African descent, and diverse women who take to the streets every day to fight for a more just, inclusive, and respectful world. She is very interested in illustration as a tool for real social change, within a society that systematically seeks to silence and continually erase all those who do not conform to what has been imposed as the norm.

**JOANNE DERTiLi, GREECE, 13** Jo is an illustrator and visual development artist from Athens, Greece. She was diagnosed with ADHD at 26, which helped her understand why a lot of things were harder for her growing up. She is passionate about raising awareness and celebrating neurodiversity in women and girls, especially autism and ADHD, since they are often overlooked.

**LILY NIE, AUSTRALIA, 17** Melbourne-based illustrator Lily Nie grew up surrounded by plants and curiosity, thanks to her plant biologist parents. Guided by her kinship with nature, her work drifts between dream and reality, exploring themes of adventure, belonging, and the quiet magic of the natural world.

**LIVELY SCOUT, AUSTRALIA, 31** Lively Scout (aka Katie Lively) is an Australian artist whose work is true to her name. Remixing eclectic influences and a love of the natural world, her work exudes energy, colour, and curiosity – creating vibrant imagery alive with story and possibility.

**LUCY ROGERS, UK, 23** Lucy is a deaf illustrator based in Oxfordshire, UK. Growing up in rural North Devon as the only deaf student in her mainstream school, Lucy discovered her love for books as a way to escape into different worlds. However, she soon realised there were no characters in those stories that reflected her experiences. This realisation inspired Lucy to become an author and artist, dedicated to creating the stories she wished she could have read as a child. To date, she has illustrated more than 15 children's books and has led various illustration workshops for young deaf people, encouraging them to explore their artistic talents.

**RUBii RED, AUSTRALiA, 19, 25** Rubii is a proud Lama Lama artist, activist, and Twitch streamer who uses her work to share her culture and discuss issues affecting her and her community. Rubii's lifelong love of anime and comic books has influenced her graphic style, in a practice that spans portraits, abstract line work, character design, and fan art.

**SAMANTHA CAMPBELL, AUSTRALIA, 21** Samantha is a contemporary artist and award-winning Illustrator. She is descended from the Dagoman people and lives in Mparntwe (Alice Springs) with her family. She draws on inspiration from her childhood experiences, nature, and community.

**SAMi BAYLY, AUSTRALiA, 9** Sami is an award-winning author and illustrator who is based in Newcastle, Australia. She loves all things weird and wonderful and enjoys painting realistic flora and fauna with watercolours. Her favourite topics tend to be the ones most people like to avoid . . . such as "ugly" animals, parasites, poo stories, and more.

**VERONiCA GUARiNO, THAiLAND, 11, 28** Veronica is a Thai-Italian illustrator, educator, and mum in Bangkok. She grew up not knowing she had ADHD and often felt out of step. Learning about her ADHD helped her understand herself in a whole new way – and she discovered that embracing it was her real superpower. Now she hopes her own journey shows children that being different is something to celebrate.

# MORE BOOKS!

For more inspiring stories about amazing women and girls, and to get tried-and-true advice on growing up and pursuing your dreams, check out other Rebel Girls books.

**SCAN FOR MORE!**

For more stories about game-changing women and girls, scan here!

**Rebel Girls**, a certified B Corporation, is a global, multi-platform empowerment brand dedicated to helping raise the most inspired and confident generation of girls. The brand purposefully creates content, products, and experiences to empower Generation Alpha girls and equip them with the knowledge and tools they need to thrive. Because confident girls will radically transform the world.

With a growing community of 43 million self-identified Rebel Girls spanning more than 115 countries, the brand engages with Gen Alpha through its book series, premier app, events, and merchandise. To date, Rebel Girls has sold more than 11 million books in 62 languages and reached 100 million digital listens/views. Award recognition includes the *New York Times* bestseller list, 2022 Apple Design Award for Social Impact, 10 Webby Awards, and more.

## JOiN THE REBEL GiRLS COMMUNiTY

Head to **rebelgirls.com** and join our email list for exclusive sneak peeks, new content drops, creative activities, and more. If you want to say hi or have any questions, email us at **hello@rebelgirls.com**. We love hearing from you.

**MORE PLACES TO FiND US!**

**Watch:** youtube.com/RebelGirls

**Listen:** rebelgirls.com/audio

**Shop:** rebelgirls.com/shop

And for your daily dose of Rebel Girls, be sure to follow us on Instagram & Facebook **@rebelgirls**